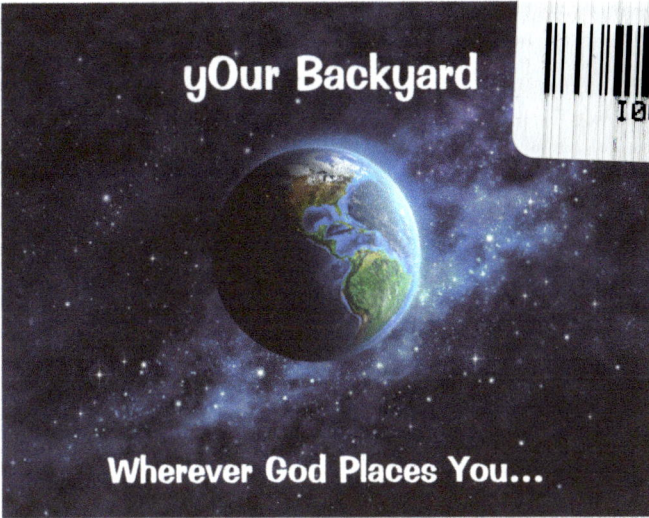

yOur Backyard

Wherever God Places You...

Welcome to yOur Backyard

yOur Backyard Magazine, part of yourbackyard.us; a quarterly online and print publication, encourages writers, actors, artists, musicians, photographers, gardeners, crafters, and youth [of all ages]. We also offer contests with the potential to be included in forthcoming issues of yOur Backyard Magazine and yOur Backyard books.

For each quarterly issue, we consider:

- Personal inspirational stories
- Poems
- Artwork
- Songs
- Photographs
- Biblical facts and/or applications

yOur Backyard's call:

And the lord said unto the servant,
Go out into the highways and hedges,
and compel them to come in,
that my house may be filled.

shELAH, editor and publisher
Email: ybymedia@gmail.com

In this Issue...

Tips...

Your car, truck,van, SUV, motorcycle, go-cart, bicycle, etc—whatever vehicle you choose to transport you from here to there, like our bodies, needs care. Take time to plan for and follow through with regular check-ups and maintenance. Like Jerry, my brother now in Heaven, who worked as a mechanic and artist said:

Take care of your car...
It will take care of you.

Velvet Queen Sunflowers with velvety crimson petals dramatically differ from the usual gold sunflowers. They serve as a distinctive dependable seed producer and mature in 100 days. It's no wonder sunflowers are so easy to grow. Goldfinches love the seeds of these majestic magnificent flowers.

Shasta Daisy Snow Lady cannot be beat for extra long, full beautiful blooms. Extra-tough in the garden, her $2^1\backslash^2$ inch; 10-12 inch tall flowers last from spring through late summer.

Emilie encourages readers: If you are not on a seed catalog list, write or email to request a seed company's or nursery's catalogs. This provides a simple way to learn the names of flowers and brighten a dreary day.

Open for Reader's Tips...

Give, and it will be given to you:
...For with the same measure that you use,
it will be measured back to you.
~ Luke 6:38

A Different Person

Jimmy Sandefur

Today, I'm a different person...

During the summer of 2015, when I came to Broadmoor [church], I was a different person than the one I am today. At that time, through my own actions, my own shortcomings and my own sins, I had grown distant from God.

Not going into details, but... my demise began with pornography and some bad choices in relationships that could have devastated my marriage if I had not stopped.

One day, sitting alone on my couch at home, I turned my face up toward Heaven and cried out to God. "God, will You please restore me? Will You bring me back to be the person I should have been?"

Several weeks earlier, I had felt drawn to Broadmoor and visited there one Sunday morning at 8:30 a.m. Because I did not feel worthy enough to be there, I sat about as far up in the balcony as you could go.

I filled out the guest card. The following week, two great guys came to my house and visited with me. They not only sat down and prayed with me, they encouraged me to come back to church and get involved.

These guys told me something I had never heard about, the "B Group." They encouraged me to become a member of this small, faith-based study group. There I found a place where I could react with men my age, men who would not judge me but who would support me through Christ's love.

I brought a Bible. I began reading my Bible again.

I started attending church every Sunday morning; sitting up in the balcony at 8:30 a.m., listening to my pastor, Dr. Chuck.

My marriage became better than ever. Anne, my wife, and I began dating again. We became friends once more. I became the father to Shelby, our beautiful daughter, that I should have been.

The way that God took someone, me, who felt so useless and worthless because of their own mistakes, amazed me. He said,

"I'm going to forget about all that. You're gonna be mine." God changed me in many ways so that I no longer was the same person as before.

Early in 2017, after I started feeling a discomfort in my chest, I scheduled an appointment with my doctor. Neither he nor I suspected my symptoms related to much of a problem. After developing bronchitis, however, I went to see a pulmonary specialist.

At that time, I still did not think much about my health problem. June 20, 2017, a day I will never forget, changed that, however. After a CT scan with more and more and more X-rays, Anne and I sat in this doctor's office waiting for the results.

When my doctor walked in and said, "Jimmy, I don't know how to tell you this...," I felt stunned. "You're 52... you're a young man by most people's standards, and—you have lung cancer.

"We've got to get you an oncologist right away."

I learned that the cancer had not only invaded my lungs, it had spread throughout my body. I began undergoing radiation treatment and chemotherapy.

When I first started back attending church, I think most people might have simply said, "That's just an average, normal, middle-aged guy. For the most part, he looks ok."

Most people did not see my spirit. They did not see my crushed soul. Physically, I appeared fine. Spiritually, I was separated from God. Now, when most people look at me, they see a person who has cancer. Although the effects of cancer as well as the radiation and the chemotherapy have weakened me, however, I am happy.

I don't have the stamina I did two years ago... But—my soul is alive. Jesus restored me. I would not trade places and go back to where I was before being diagnosed with lung cancer. I could not have handled the news about my sickness then. I'm thankful that God made me a different person...

I am thankful that in God's loving, caring, amazing grace and reconstruction of my life, He saw me. He not only saw me, He ran to me. He picked me up and brought me back to Himself.

I'm thankful for that... I thank God that today because of Jesus Christ, I'm a different person.

Excerpt from **On this Side of Heaven...** (to be published)

"C" the Way to Reach Your Goals...

1. **Clear away the clutter in your thoughts** to begin to see a clearer picture of your goal in your mind's eye. Writing down your goals will help clarify them. Someone said, when you can't write down your goals, they are not clear enough. Unwritten goals are more likely to be out of focus or overlooked.

2. **Collect what you need to begin to take the steps needed to reach your goal.** Just like you need a map to know how to make a trip, you need to map out your plans to arrive at your goal. Begin to save money you will need. Devote time and energy to making your plan materialize.

3. **Cultivate the right kind of confidence.** David's confidence to fight Goliath increased as he reviewed God's past record. David told Goliath, "You come to me with a spear and... I come to you in the name of the Lord." Remember the battle is the Lord's. Trust that with God's help, we, as His children can do everything He calls us to do. He's responsible to provide the way...

4. **Continue on a courageous course of action.** David planned his fight by listening to and observing Goliath. He insured he had the right "ammunition." While he listened to Goliath boast and threaten, David stood strong, "faithing" in our Heavenly Father's power. David had Goliath off guard as the giant snickered at the thought of being threatened by a little runt like David.

5. **Confirm progress on a calendar.** Set and meet deadlines. To counter procrastination, rather than repeating, "One of these days...," write target dates on a calendar. If you miss one target, reschedule. Practice what you know to do.

6. **Cultivate cooperation from friends, family and those who have "made it" to where you plan to go.** Make a habit of helping those who need help, as well as asking for help. and support from others. Not many goals can be accomplished without help. When you share..., it becomes "We..."

7. **Continue to be Consistent.** Once you prayerfully set your eyes on a goal within God's will, don't let anyone steal your dream. Don't let the cares of this world blur your vision. Cultivate and practice an attitude of stick-to-it-ism.

Snowmen with Different Hearts

For Ages 3 - 103

Snowman Coloring idea: www.RaisingOurKids.com

Name: _____	
Address: _____	
_____	
Phone #: _____ **Age:** _____	

Through My Worst Moments
Beverly June (Daily) Stewart

If I don't get to that exit soon, I'm going to have to pull over and and stop, I thought. Prior to the flood, driving on Interstate 40 did not bother me. That day, however, being penned in behind an 18-wheeler, I panicked.

Earlier this year, following the horrific flood August 21, 2021, where I lived in Waverly, Tennessee, I prayed through my tears. "Lord, please help me. Just help me... please. I don't know how I can go on..."

Some days, I felt like I did not want to go on living. Sometimes, when experiencing a panic attack, I not only felt out of control, but wondered why God did not instantly answer me.

"What am I going to do?" I cried. "God, you took Ken away from me. And now everything else is gone. Why? Why?"

I did not understand why in 1980, a drunk driver driving on the wrong side of the interstate hit my family head-on, killing all of them, my parents and my brother... Then, Ken, my husband for the past six years, had died seven months before the flood that destroyed our house.

Before my family died, I had been engaged to Ken in 1977-78. We broke up, however, and did not see each other again until 2013. After we married in 2014, we were inseparable. And then, as he experienced problems with his blood sugar, Ken's health started to decline. A wound on his heel, from Ken scraping off part of his skin when putting on his shoe, would not heal. Even after surgery, the wound stubbornly worsened. Then the injury went septic.

Ken started throwing up blood the Sunday before he died that following Tuesday. After I had cleaned him up and given him a second dose of morphine, I smiled and squeezed his hand as he said, "Thank you, Babe... Thank you for taking care of me. I love you."

Ken died January 27, 2021.

Although I hated seeing Ken suffer, and knew he was ready to go, my world as I had known it came to an end. When Saturday morning, August 21, 2021, dawned, weathermen warned that strong storms were possible. I decided to go to my neighbor's house to ride out the threatening weather. There, her son was moving their vehicles in case the creek behind their house flooded. I walked up to their door with clear rain water up to my ankles.

And then...

Without warning, a more than eight-foot-tall wall of water came rolling down the vacant lot beside my neighbor's house. When I looked across the street to where I lived, I saw the carport at the end of my garage collapse. By this time, the water flooded in under my neighbor's front door and the back. Her refrigerator fell over. Before we could pull the attic stairway down, water had risen above my waist.

As we climbed up the attic stairway, the water continued to rise. Two young men I knew rescued us on a jet ski. My heart sank when I saw what was left of the house Ken and I had lived in.

I had my Job [biblical] moment... I screamed out to God, "You took Ken away from me. And now..."

This January, on the one-year anniversary of Ken's death, I again walked over the three-fourths of now cleared acreage where Ken and I had lived. This time, I noticed an open book lying on the foundation of what used to be a carport.

I picked up the Bible. The pages from the book of Genesis in the front through Exodus were gone. The flood waters had left the books in the back of the Bible spotted, soiled, and stuck together. I stared amazed, however, where the Bible had folded open to Jeremiah 29:11. The NIV translates this verse as: "For I know the plans I have for you," declares the LORD, "plans to prosper you and not to harm you, plans to give you hope and a future."

That day, God lovingly reassured me that He had not forgotten me. His Word reminded me that even when I may panic; even when flood waters rise, He has a plan and will see me through. He holds my future and gives me hope.

**These things I have spoken unto you,
that in me ye might have peace.
In the world ye shall have tribulation:
but be of good cheer; I have overcome the world.**
~ John 16:33

Thoughts of Courage for the New Year

Martin Luther: As wisdom without courage is futile, even so faith without hope is nothing worth; for hope endures and overcomes misfortune and evil.

William Feather: Here is the secret of inspiration. Tell yourself that thousands and tens of thousands of people, not very intelligent and certainly no more intelligent than the rest of us, have mastered problems as difficult as those that now baffle you.

Plato: We are twice armed if we fight with faith.

Dale Carnegie: Today is life... the only life you are sure of. Make the most of today. Get interested in something. Shake yourself awake. Develop a hobby. Let the winds of enthusiasm sweep through you. Live today with gusto.

In Matthew 10: 28 – 31, Jesus' words reassure: And do not fear those who kill the body but cannot kill the soul. But rather fear Him who is able to destroy both soul and body in hell. Are not two sparrows sold for a copper coin? And not one of them falls to the ground apart from your Father's will. But the very hairs of your head are all numbered. Do not fear therefore; you are of more value than many sparrows.

Paul wrote in Romans 8:38 – 39: For I am convinced that nothing can ever separate us from his love. Death can't, and life can't. The angels won't, and all the powers of hell itself cannot keep God's love away. Our fears for today, our worries about tomorrow, or where we are—high above the sky, or in the deepest ocean—nothing will ever be able to separate us from the love of God demonstrated by our Lord Jesus Christ when he died for us.

**Now
faith is the substance
of things hoped for,
the evidence
of things not seen.**
~Hebrews 11:1

From Hating the Cross to Preaching It

Luke Hockenjos

"Even though I had a black and white Cross tattooed on my right arm's upper bicep, I hated *the Cross* ...

"If I had known you, I would have hated you," Luke, a 32-year-old former drug dealer, now preacher evangelist, told me. "At that time in my life, I only saw *the Cross* as a a tattoo...

"I hated everything. Many who knew me saw me as a hateful individual. My mom and dad raised me in a "good" home with mom, a professing Christian, ensuring that she, my sister, and I attended church regularly—Sunday morning... Sunday night... Wednesday night...revival... Vacation Bible School.

"I chose a *Cross* for my first tattoo because I thought Mom, more a fan of tattoos than piercings, would like it. She had agreed that I could get a tattoo if I made the A&B honor roll at school. Somehow, I did...

"I don't remember much prayer in our home," he said.

When banned from school for a year for "threatening" another student, Luke worked as his dad's helper in a welding business. He started drinking alcohol at the age of 15, but by 21, Luke was drinking heavily, using meth (methamphetamine), and abusing whatever illegal drugs he could get his hands on.

In 2010, Luke dropped out of college and went to work in the oilfield. He re-enrolled in college in 2013, but quickly dropped out again. As he hung out with people into that lifestyle of using illegal drugs, especially one of his closest friends, Luke started selling...

"I was in a dark place," Luke said.

Although Luke lived away from home, his mom did his laundry. One day, he discovered that she had put a Bible beneath his folded clothes at the bottom of the laundry basket. The Bible was an old one he had sometimes read when a teenager. Luke started reading Proverbs 11:1, "A false balance is abomination to the Lord: but a just weight is his delight." He thought: *As long as I keep my scales accurate, I can use and still sell drugs.*

In October 2014, the daughter of a preacher in Ruston, Louisiana, invited him to attend church where his mother had taken him in the past. "We miss you..." the text read. "We would love to see you."

The last thing Luke expected was for anybody to want him at church.

That next Sunday morning when Luke attended the service, he expected people to say something negative about the way he was dressed, wearing a bandana and shorts. Instead, those who met him welcomed him and hugged his neck. He heard words he had not heard in a long, long, long time, "Good to see you..."

Luke's mom still attended this church and did not know Luke would be there. "What is that on your head?" she asked. The next Sunday, however, when Luke's mom sat next to him in church, she wore a bandana. Even though Luke was well-known in public as a crystal meth drug addict and dealer, the preacher and others Christians showed they loved him. They even took Luke out to eat with them each Sunday.

During this time, Luke said, "I was pretty out there." Driving on one of his darkest days, feeling fed up with life, Luke grabbed his truck's steering wheel and yelled out, "God if You are real, show Yourself... "Satan if you're real, show yourself... Whichever one of you wants me—come get me... I'll be loyal."

The next day Luke heard Michael Frances, a former Columbia mob leader, share his story. Michael said that while he served time in prison, somebody gave him a Bible. Through this and other experiences, Michael surrendered his life to Jesus. That day, Luke said that he wanted the same Jesus Michael talked about.

Driving away from the church, on the main road, a middle-aged man cut Luke off in traffic and flipped him off. Luke chased the man, driving 120 mph. The offending driver turned onto a service road, speeding ahead. A red light unexpectedly stopped him.

Luke drove the nose of his truck into the door of the offender's 2000 Chevy, intending to push him off the adjoining bridge. Before he could do so, Luke's truck abruptly stopped. It refused to budge.

That's when the atmosphere inside Luke's truck changed. "Son," Luke said he heard a voice plainly say, "This isn't the plan I have for you."

When Luke put his truck in reverse, it moved. When he later read Jeremiah 29:11, he knew that he had a future purpose and hope in Jesus.

"Until that day during that dark time in my life," Luke said, "I did not realize just how lost and broken I was, nor did I know that I so desperately needed a Savior." Today, Luke encourages others to trust God's gift of Jesus Christ, the reason Christians celebrate Christmas.

Luke reminds others of the message in John 3:17 "For God sent not his Son into the world to condemn the world; but that the world through him might be saved." *The Cross*, even if a person hates it, as Luke did in his past, represents God's great love for us. Now, as Luke shares how Jesus saved and changed him, he tells others, "Today, the cross means everything to me…"

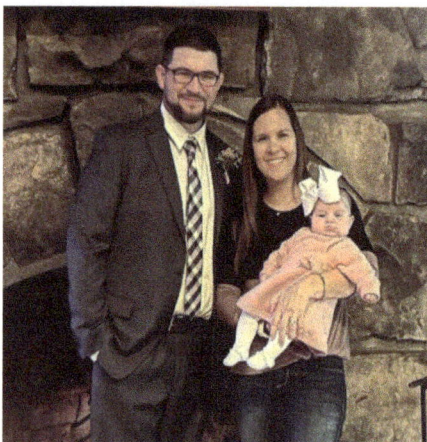

For the preaching of the cross
is to them that perish foolishness;
but unto us which are saved
it is the power of God.
~1 Corinthians 1:18

Inspiring Good Courage

A well-known bull fighter:
Be courageous.
To fight a bull when you are not scared is nothing.
And not to fight a bull when you are scared is nothing.
But to fight a bull when you are scared—that is something.

Anonymous:
He that loses money loses little,
he that loses health loses much,
but he that loses courage loses all.

Ralph Waldo Emerson:
They can conquer who believe they can...
He has not learned the first lesson of life
who does not every day surmount a fear.

Proverbs in Old Testament:
If thou faint in the day of adversity,
thy strength is small ~ Proverbs 24:10.

Dale Carnegie:
If you want to conquer fear, don't think about yourself.
Try to help others, and your fears will vanish.

Publilius Syrus:
Courage comes by being brave:
fear comes by holding back.

Theodore Roosevelt:
There were all sorts of things I feared,
from grizzly bears to mean horses and gun-fighters;
but by acting as if I was not afraid
I gradually ceased to be afraid.

Have not I commanded thee?
Be strong and of a good courage;
be not afraid,
neither be thou dismayed:
for the Lord thy God is with thee
whithersoever thou goest.
~ Joshua 1:9

Music — Then

John Henry Newton, Jr. (1725-1807) former slaveship captain, "born again" to become an evangelist.

Roots of *Amazing Grace's* first verse grew from the story of the Prodigal Son that Luke recorded. The father said, " For this my son was dead, and is alive again; he was lost, and is found. And they began to be merry" (Luke 15:24). Newton used the words "I was blind but now I see" from Jesus healing a blind man who told the Pharisees that he could now see (John 9). Newton declared "Oh to grace how great a debtor!" In "Amazing Grace," and in his diary entries and letters.

Amazing grace! (how sweet the sound)
That sav'd a wretch like me!
I once was lost, but now am found,
Was blind, but now I see.

'Twas grace that taught my heart to fear,
And grace my fears reliev'd;
How precious did that grace appear
The hour I first believ'd!

Thro' many dangers, toils, and snares,
I have already come;
'Tis grace hath brought me safe thus far,
And grace will lead me home.

The Lord has promis'd good to me,
His word my hope secures;
He will my shield and portion be
As long as life endures.

Yes, when this flesh and heart shall fail,
And mortal life shall cease;
I shall possess, within the veil,
A life of joy and peace.

The earth shall soon dissolve like snow,
The sun forbear to shine;
But God, who call'd me here below,
Will be forever mine.
~ John Newton, 1779

Music — Now

My favorite song that I've written? That's a tough one. I've written dozens and dozens of songs. I wrote one of my favorites, *Love in the Trenches* in 1985.

I usually write when I'm inspired. Sometimes, I'll sit down and try to write. I'm regularly jotting down thoughts and phrases along the way.

Dan Smith

Throw the First Stone

Go ahead and throw it if you never stumbled.
Go ahead and throw it
If you've never fallen from grace yourself.
Go ahead and throw it
If your life's never crumbled at any time
Go ahead and throw it... be the first in line.

Chorus:
Throw the first stone if you've never stolen or lied.
Throw the first stone if you've never been full of pride.
If you've never given into lust or greed
If you've never taken more than you really need.

Look'a here who's that pointing their finger at me
Is their vision so obstructed that they cannot see
The things that they're doin'?
Well, you know they're wrong too
We've been blind for so long.
Why don't we throw the first stone?

**So when they continued asking him,
he [Jesus] lifted up himself, and said unto them,
He that is without sin among you,
let him first cast a stone at her.**
~ John 8:7

God's Not [Only] American
Dan Smith

When you're dealing drugs—you're always in trouble with the law. I know. At one time, I lived that life. Police in town knew who I was. They knew my name.

My birth dad left my mom before I was born. When I was 7-years-old, my mom married my stepdad, a brutal man who abused me verbally and physically. My stepfather, a policeman, was also a thief. While I was growing up, my step dad, who also abused alcohol and drugs, brutally beat me more times than I like to remember. He would use his police belt and just about anything and in any way he could think of to inflict pain.

I started using drugs when I was 12. In 1975, during the "hippie phase," before I left home at the age of 17, I began "work" as a drug dealer. By this time, I was finally big enough to defend myself against my step dad. Several years, after I left home at the age of 17, my stepdad drank himself to death.

At 21, when I first heard that Jesus Christ gave His life to save mine, I didn't accept this news right away. One day, as the Lord convicted my heart, I knew, It's time to make a decision... That day, I prayed, "Lord, please forgive me. Come into my heart..." He did.

One moment, my life was going the wrong way, and then, boom; it started moving the other direction—the right way.

Even after I became a Christian, and my life started moving in the right direction, however, I remained angry at my stepdad for a long time. He had been dead 10 years when I realized I had come to the point I needed to forgive him for abusing me. It wasn't easy; I had to wrestle with doing this.

The Lord helped me. He helped me realize I didn't know my stepdad as a person. I only knew he lived in a defensive world. I didn't know what made him the way he was. I just knew he didn't know the Lord. There was no clear reason for the anger in his life.

Not long after I forgave my step dad, God began giving me songs to write. One particular song, *God's Not American*, however, still speaks to my heart. I encourage others to remember that although God loves the Red, White and Blue—He's not American. Our Heavenly Father is not American; not Iranian; not Canadian. He's Who He is—He's God.

Hair

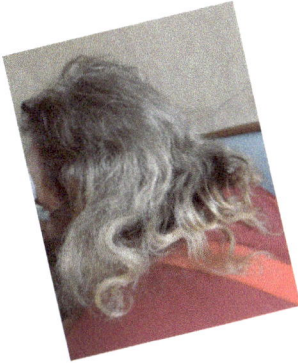

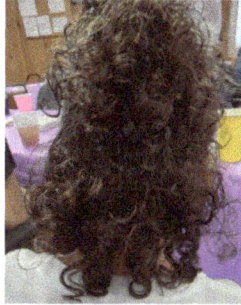

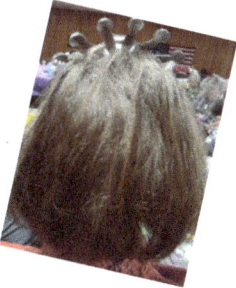

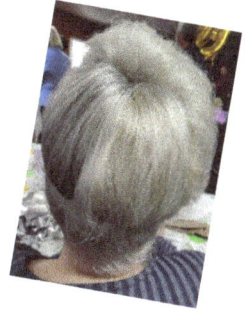

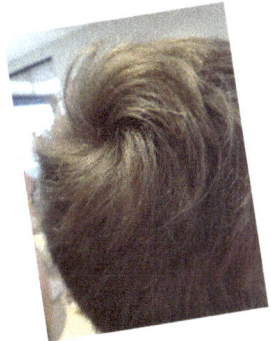

But the very hairs of your head
are all numbered.

~ Matthew 10:30

Bible Crossword Puzzle

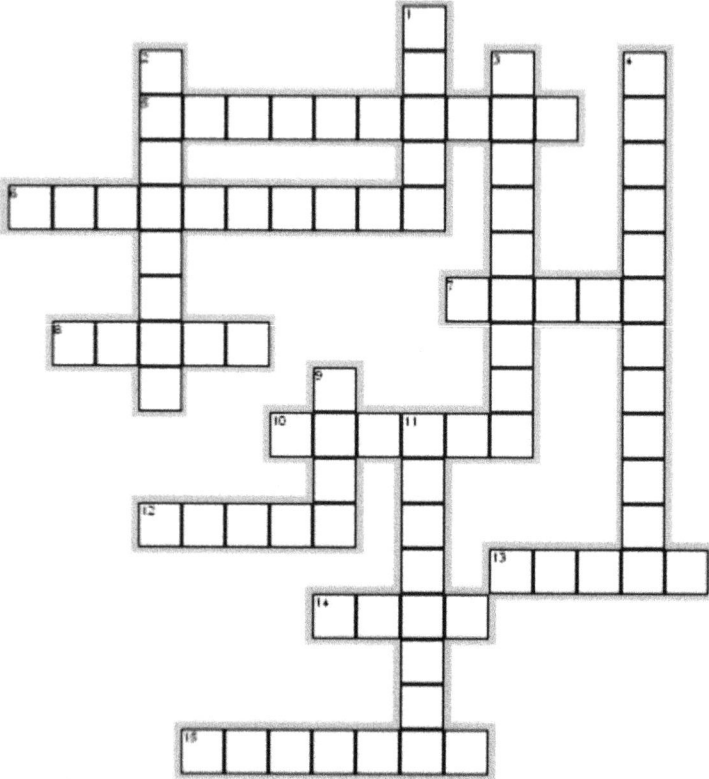

Across

5. David described himself being this way when old.
6. With God, nothing is _____.
7. When to seek "the kingdom of God and His righteousness."
8. Eat this "because it is good."
10. Jesus said to do this to invite others to His house.
12. When we do this, we see that the Lord is good.
13. Describes what kind of mind God gives us.
14. Do this with those who are crying.
15. When we give, we are more this than when we receive something.

Down

1. What Jesus left His children.
2. In 1 Corinthians, 12:1, Paul wrote he would not have us to be this word.
3. Describes the feet of those who preach the gospel of peace.
4. Jesus is this for our sins.
9. A new commandment Jesus gave us to do to one another.
11. This word in David's prayer is also a term used in canning.

Answers on page 46

With God, We Can...

Tyler Sandefur

"He's the fat one..."

Tyler said that's what others said about him growing up as an overweight, insecure child. Years ago, Tyler not only struggled with being overweight but also hurt by the harsh, hurtful words others aimed at him. Too often, someone would refer to him as "the fat one," he said, "Other negative names I regularly heard growing up, included 'Jelly Roll;' 'Fatty' 'Chubs...' I was repeatedly called these insulting names, as well as some others I could not imagine. No child nor adult should have to go through that experience."

Tyler recalls:

Hands down, growing up an overweight child had to be one of the most difficult times in my life. At that time, however, I referred to myself as "husky." Rather than realizing I was actually a medically obese guy at 5'6", weighing 194 pounds; walking around with 30%+ body fat, I was in denial about myself and my unhealthy eating habits.

Sometimes, I woke up wondering, *how did I, of all people, become this epitome of adolescent unhealthy living?*

When I finally sat down and thought about what had made me become obese, I realized it was not just one thing, but a culmination of factors. I watched too much TV. My diet was not only unhealthy but fattening and lacking the nutrients I needed. I did not exercise regularly.

On an average school day, I would come home to an empty house to find a fully stocked refrigerator, an empty couch, and an X-box 360. Every afternoon after school, I would set my backpack right inside my bedroom door, and instead of completing my homework, I would head straight to the kitchen and make whatever sounded like a good choice. For example, a favorite snack of mine would include Dr Pepper, potato chips, and a huge slice of cake Mom had just freshly baked. I did not care what the flavor of the cake nor the kind of foods I ate. I only wanted what tasted good.

In addition to making poor food choices, I developed another bad habit of disregarding my stomach when it would tell me I was full. No matter how much food I put on my plate, I felt obligated to eat every bite. I was not only eating unhealthily when I got home from school, I routinely started every morning the same. When I woke up, if my mom was not home before I caught the bus to school, my unhealthy approach to food was *do whatever I wanna do because I feel like it* mentality. For breakfast, I might eat leftover Chinese food or pizza from the night before with a soft drink on the side. If I had any potato chips left over, I might help myself to three or more servings. After breakfast at shower time, when I took my shirt off and looked at myself in the mirror, I felt disgusted with what I saw. I could not stand the person I saw in the mirror. My image, however, reflected the choices I had been living.

Two years later, I decided to adopt the lifestyle I live today; one that I am proud of. Along with making healthy choices pertaining to food, I began to work out every day after school. When several "friends" told me, "Man, you can't lose weight," I determined that with God's help, I would do what they told me could not be done.

Two years later, I decided to adopt the lifestyle I live today; one that I am proud of. Along with making healthy choices pertaining to food, I began to work out every day after school. When several "friends" told me, "Man, you can't lose weight," I determined that with God's help, I would do what they told me could not be done.

I adopted boxing as my passion and with the help of my coach, I made a complete physical transformation. At first, boxing served as just a way to lose weight. I soon realized that like a number of teenagers, I had a lot of anger and stress that needed to be released. For me, punching something turned out to be the perfect release.

Every afternoon after training, instead of reaching for a soda, I reached for water and a piece of fruit or some other healthy alternative to cake and chips. I quickly learned that I needed both aspects of my new lifestyle to stay in shape; exercise and eating right.

As I saw the numbers on the scales begin to drop and started to slim down, I found it easy to stay motivated. I realized that the only person who could stop me from getting in shape would be me.

I know that I could not have made such a change within my own strength. My changes were only possible through the strength and wisdom God gave me. I am thankful to have come from an insecure, overweight child to an athletic young man with a newfound sense of motivation and self-worth.

Today, I no longer see myself as "the fat one..."

shELAH's Endnote:

Tyler's story reminds me of Luke 18: 27 (NLT): "What is impossible from a human perspective is possible with God."

As our Heavenly Father gives us opportunities, may we offer others what Peter told Jesus that He had, "...words of eternal life." In doing this, instead of blurting out insensitive, harsh words or judging others, we will hopefully, prayerfully share what we say in love. We will encourage and remind one another that with God, we can do what needs doing.

The thief cometh not, but for to steal,
and to kill, and to destroy:
I am come that they might have life,
and that they might have it more abundantly.
~ John 10:10

Forever Friends

Sometimes in life you find
A special friend,
Someone who changes your life
Just by being a part of it.
Someone who makes you laugh
Until you can't stop;
That there really is good in the world.
Someone who convinces you that
There really is an unlocked door
Just waiting for you to open it.

When you're down and the world
Seems dark and empty,
Your forever friend lifts you up
In spirit and makes that dark and empty
World suddenly seem bright and full.

Your forever friend gets you through
The hard times, the sad times
And confusing times.
If you turn and walk away,
Your forever friend follows.
If you lose your way,
Your forever friend guides you
And cheers you on.
Your forever friend holds your hand
And tells you that
Everything is going to be okay.

And if you find such a friend,
You feel happy and complete,
Because you need not worry;
You have a forever friend -
And forever has no end...

♡

Letter from a Civil War Soldier

Port Hudson, LA   March 30, '63 (1863)

My dear wife,

I received ...letters dated March 16th & 20th, written while you were at Mt. Fenny, the one at "Home" the one dated 20th. I am glad to learn that you have been so well and enjoyed your visit in the country though I fear for the children on account of the measles, the bags of asaschita will do them no good—it is an old woman's remedy.

This letter I feel will be very uninteresting as I feel very little like writing. It is a very cold, windy day and very unpleasant. I assure you have had some very hot weather until the last few days. I don't see the reason you get so few letters from me as I write every other day when I know the way is open. Sometimes the bridges between Clinton and Camp Moore are washed away ...when our mail communications are cut off. I have written in former letters of this and of my frequent letter writing but you don't seem to understand the difficulties under which we labor here in this out of the way place. I hope you will not belabor me anymore until you find out if I deserve it or not. I used to blame you in the same way until I was better informed. You have no idea how I felt when I would hear the letters of the company called over and did not hear my name announced. I thought all sort of hard things against you.

...You speak about the anniversary of our marriage and whether I had forgotten it. No my Dear I had not forgotten it but knew not how to write about it.

My pants fit me to a te. I mean the English cloth ones you bought from St. Zardoc. The box you sent my McRae has not arrived and I am fearful will never find me. I would very much like to write to Cathie but I have the time really just now. I will try and write your father next mail if I possibly can.

... I would like very much to send some sugar but there is no chance, only when somebody is going from here home. And they always have as much as they can carry for themselves... It is worth twenty cts per pound and syrup about one dollar a gal. My dear wife I feel so little like writing that I am almost tempted not to send this home but you must overlook this...

Oh that I had you in my arms how I would caress you. Great God, will the time ever come when this infernal war will end? I must close... Give my love to your Father and Mother, and kiss our little ones for me...pray that the time may soon come when we can meet once more.

Your devoted,

Harville
Andrew Harville Beauchamp
Company F, 1st Alabama Infantry

Note from Jimmy Sandefur, contributor of this letter:

Beauchamp was stationed at Port Hudson—about 30 miles north of Baton Rouge, Louisiana. Along with Vicksburg, this fort protected the Mississippi River and Confederate shipping. Under siege for months, the fort's conditions deteriorated to where soldiers ate rats and horses to survive. Vicksburg surrendered on July 4th, 1863 and Port Hudson surrendered five days later. Union soldiers captured and imprisoned Beauchamp. When later paroled, he rejoined his unit and fought the rest of the war. He survived and returned home to his "dear wife" and children. ♡

In 1936, an unknown photographer took this picture of Arkansan Confederate veteran William M. Cantrell (about 88; 1847–1937) with his wife Maudie (about 21; 1914–2008). Maudie Hopkins, a Civil War widow, 1936 photograph of Arkansan Confederate veteran. William M. Cantrell (about 88; 1847–1937) Maudie Hopkins was one of the few Civil War widows to survive into the 21st century.

Where's Your Heart in The Big Picture?

*Clint Clarneau as told to shELAH

God, if You are God... if You are real—why is all this bad stuff happening to me? Why do we have wars? Diseases? Kids dying? Divorce? At one time in my life, as these questions haunted me; I was the loser of losers.

While I questioned if God existed, nothing seemed to be going right in my life. I thought I'd always been a Christian. But one day, a music director of a church I'd visited, rode his motorcycle to where I was lettering a truck. He looked into my eyes and told me what Jesus said to Nicodemus years ago, "You must be born again."

In the "big picture," in the realm of eternity, my heart wasn't right. I realized Jesus paid for my sins... that I could be born again and by grace through faith in Jesus Christ, have eternal life. The night I heard this news, I couldn't wait to pray. I fell on my knees and like the thief on the other side of the cross when Jesus was crucified, my heart cried out, "Lord, please save me..."

Today, as I paint pictures and share how Christ gave His life so we could be born again, I know the answer to the questions that hounded me. Sin. From God's word, I learned sin is the root of all suffering. Man and his sin created the suffering we experience in life. That does not necessarily mean a person who suffers does so because of their personal sin, but, in general, sin causes suffering.

Sin first entered our world when Adam and Eve disobeyed God in the Garden of Eden. The 10 Commandments clearly depict God's laws. Jesus said that He did not come to destroy the law, but fulfill it. He taught His followers that anger and lust, along with other sins that lurk inside our hearts, in a very real sense, break the 10 Commandments. When Jesus went to the cross, He showed how far He was willing to go to save us from sin. His dying said, "Yes, sin causes suffering, but I'm willing to suffer and die for your sins."

Before I trusted Christ as my Savior, I thought I was a good person. The closer I came to Christ, however, the more I realized my need for God's forgiveness, for His grace in my life. Each time I paint a 13-foot canvas and share the gospel, I encourage those watching to look beyond their lives today. I stress, "Don't only plan where you will live now, but in eternity. Consider how you fit into God's 'big picture.'"

Where's You Heart
In God's Big Picture?

...like the thief
on the other side
of the cross
When Jesus
was crucified,
my heart cried,
"Lord,
please save me..."

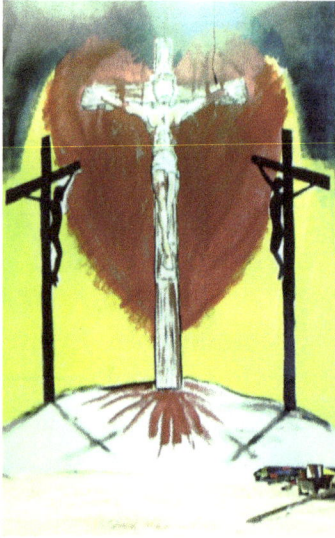

"I'm willing
to suffer and die
for your sins..."
Jesus' death
said that... and
more.

When Jesus
went to the cross,
He showed
how far
He was willing to go
to save us
from sin.

♡

*Clint Clarneau, a painter/artist/author, who Lives in Shelbyville, Tennessee, paints signs to earn a living. He "lives," however, to share the gospel message through his art and presentations to groups.

...You must be born again.
~ John 3:7

Move It or Lose It...

Dr. Scott Jutte

(Excerpt from forthcoming book, *Better Health, Simple as THAT*)

You would think that they would have had their stuff together.

That thought came to Scotty's mind nine years ago when "Sam," an educated, prominent person in his community, had her small compact car towed into his auto repair shop.

"My timing belt broke...," Sam told Scotty. "I was traveling along and then my car just quit. I had it towed to my house and then to your shop."

What Sam failed to tell Scotty, however, complicated the challenge to get her car going again. What she did not tell him would have saved them both time and frustration.

Scotty phoned and told Sam, "Right now, your bill is $1300. When your timing belt broke, it hit your engine's valves and damaged them. Even though you've practically got a new engine, and your car fires, it won't start. Exactly how long has your car been having problems?"

"My timing belt broke about a year ago...," Sam admitted. "My car's just been sitting in my yard since I had it towed back then."

"During that time your car sat stagnating," I told Sam, "some animal, maybe a chipmunk, chewed through some of your wires so I had to replace them. And, we had to install a new battery. The one in your car has been long dead."

"How much more will all this cost?" Sam asked.

"I don't know just yet," I admitted. "I have to get it running and then will let you know if anything else needs to be repaired. Letting your car sit for a year created more problems than your timing belt breaking."

Sam, like many customers who bring their vehicles to Scotty for repairs, failed to do what their owner's manual dictates—take them to a mechanic for regular preventative maintenance. This neglect not only increases the likelihood of expensive repairs, it can put the vehicle's driver, as well as others on the road, in danger.

Scotty confirms what I've been told: that it's harder on your

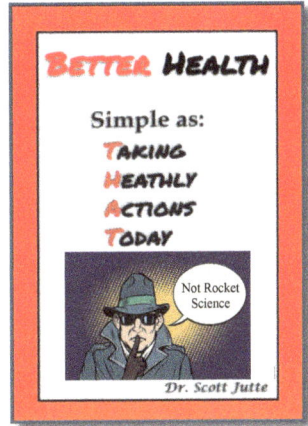

vehicle to let it sit than it is to drive it regularly. Likewise, with our bodies. Matt Whitehead, an Egoscue University certified Postural Alignment Specialist and Advanced Exercise Therapist, as well as a wanna-be slam dunk champion, admits that the phrase, "move it or lose it" means one needs to exercise regularly to maintain fitness.

Walking, one of the best physical activities for exercise, doesn't require specialized equipment or training. It may be done virtually anywhere, any time, and at any pace. Walking works all your muscles, not just your legs.

Unfortunately, like Sam with her car, too many people neglect walking. They fail to move their bodies regularly. Instead, some simply sit stagnant until they deteriorate too much to start...

You would think that today with the access we have to health information, especially in this manual, we would have our stuff together...

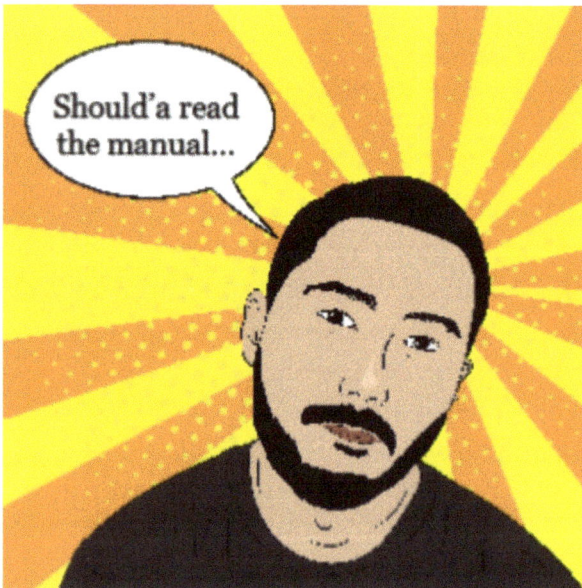

When we think about it,
while we still have our health—
we can...

Love A'int Giving Up

"What kind of gift do you call this?" Bethany yelled at Barbara, her mom.

The struggle between Barbara, and Bethany, her 21-year-old daughter, reached its zenith when Bethany was arrested for DUI. For several weeks afterwards, Bethany and Barbara did not speak.

Two weeks later, when they met for lunch, Barbara handed Bethany a small wrapped gift. Bethany pursed her lips and flippantly opened the box. When she saw the small rock inside, she rolled her dark brown eyes.

"What's this? A rock? You gave me a rock!" she smirked.

Barbara touched Bethany's hand. "Read the card," she said.

"This rock is thousands of years old. That's how long it will take before I give up on you," Bethany read.

Tears streamed down Bethany's cheeks as she reached over and hugged Barbara.

In an even greater sense, our Heavenly Father breaks through to us with His unrelenting, enduring love. He not only gave His only begotten Son, Jesus Christ, to die on the cross to pay the penalty for our sins to reconcile us to Him, as David recounts in Psalm 18, He is our rock.

**The Lord is my rock,
and my fortress,
and my deliverer;
my God, my strength,
in whom I will trust;
my buckler,
and the horn of my salvation,
and my high tower.**
~ Psalm 18:2

Unleavened Bread

Ingredients:

1¾ cups unbleached flour
¼ cup whole wheat flour
1 teaspoon pink Himalayan salt
1 tablespoon olive oil
¾ cup warm water

Directions:

➢ Add dry ingredients to a bowl, Stir to mix well.

➢ Pour olive oil and warm water into blended dry ingredients.

➢ Form mixture into small balls. If dough feels sticky/too wet, add flour; if it appears too dry, add a bit more warm water.

➢ Divide dough into equal portions and form into balls.

➢ Roll each dough ball out into ¼ inch flat breads.

➢ Use fork to poke a few holes in each dough ball.

➢ Heat a seasoned cast iron skillet over a medium high heat.

➢ Cook each flat bread 4 to 5 minutes on each side.

**And Jesus said unto them,
am the bread of life...**
~John 6:35

Cake Mix Cookies

Ingredients:

1 box of cake mix—your choice

½ cup vegetable oil, canola oil, or 7 tablespoons butter, melted

2 large eggs.

Optional: ¾ cup mix-ins such as M&Ms, pecans, coconut, chocolate chips, or candy pieces.

May also top cookies with sprinkles before baking or ice them afterwards.

Directions:

> ➢ Pre-heat oven to 350°F.

> ➢ Prepare baking sheet with parchment paper. This will help prevent the bottom of cookies from burning.

> ➢ Use a mixer to blend the first 3 ingredients together in a large bowl. Mix until the dough becomes smooth. Add extra mix-ins. At this time, blend mix ins into dough or later, after forming dough into cookies, top each cookie with mix-ins. Refrigerating the mixed dough for at least an hour will make it easier to work with.

> ➢ Use a cookie scoop to position the dough onto a prepared baking sheet.

> ➢ Bake in preheated oven for 9 to 11 minutes until the cookies are firm but still soft.

Achy Breaky Cake

Cyrus—the Artist
formerly known as Billy Ray Cyrus

1 package yellow cake mix
1 can sweetened, condensed milk
1 small bottle caramel sauce
16 ounce container Cool Whip®
2 large Butterfinger® bars, crushed

> Bake cake mix according to package directions in a 9 x 13 inch pan.

> When cooled, poke numerous holes in cake with a straw.

> Combine milk and caramel sauce until smooth and pour over cooled cake.

> Ice cake with Cool Whip® and sprinkle crushed Butterfingers® over the top.
> Keep refrigerated.

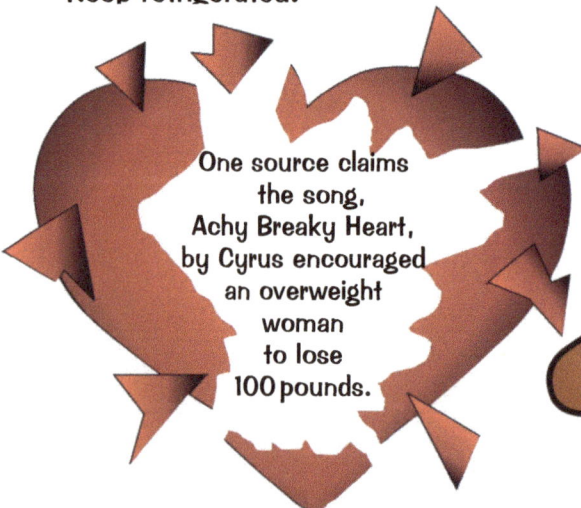

One source claims the song, Achy Breaky Heart, by Cyrus encouraged an overweight woman to lose 100 pounds.

Words from and about "The Word"

Long before scientists confirmed the following facts of nature, the Bible recorded:

- ➢ Roundness of the earth **(Isaiah 40:22)**
- ➢ Almost infinite extent of the sidereal universe **(Isaiah 55:9)**
- ➢ Law of conservation of mass and energy **(II Peter 3:7)**
- ➢ Hydrologic cycle **(Ecclesiastes 1:7)**
- ➢ Vast number of stars **(Jeremiah 33:22)**
- ➢ Law of increasing entropy (**Psalm 102:25**)
- ➢ Importance of blood in life processes **(Leviticus 17:11)**
- ➢ Atmospheric circulation **(Ecclesiastes 1:6)**
- ➢ Gravitational field **(Job 26:7)**

No archaeological finding discredits a biblical reference.

Isaiah predicted Christ's birthplace, as well as His death place, and the way He would die. The book of Isaiah records how much money would be paid to betray Christ.

More than 40 different authors wrote the Holy Bible over 1,500 years at different times in history. Although enemies have attacked this book more than any other, it has amazingly survived. In the book, *Evidence that Demands A Verdict,* Josh McDowell wrote:

> From the days of the Roman emperors to present day communist countries, it [the Holy Bible] has been the target of complete annihilation and continues to thrive in readership and reference. (Amazing for a book that merely teaches submission to governing authorities, goodwill toward your fellow man and personal diligence). Not only do all authors agree on the same subject, unlike any other great work, they are painfully frank about their shortcomings and failures.

Every word of God is pure;
He is a shield
to those who put their trust in Him.
~ Proverbs 30:5

Arvin's Art

I can't even look at a sunset right... Arvin thought. "At one time in my past," he said. "I did not even know how to enjoy the beauty of a sunset. In turn, I tunneled even deeper into my mental pit of depression; thinking that neither I nor the art I created, could ever be good enough.

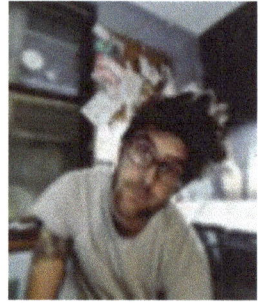

"For years, even growing up, I felt off-center. As a child of a military family, I moved 14 times during my formative years. My roots felt like those of a tumbleweed... somewhere yet non-existent. Art helped save my sanity."

According to Arvin, his growth from thinking like a "wann-a-be" artist, constantly criticizing himself and his work, to "being" a real artist took time. Despite his phobias and fears of messing up a blank canvas, he started to fill dead, empty spaces with samplings of life. As he regularly confronted his fears painting, drawing, and illustration, despite making mistakes, he began to learn how to appreciate both himself and his art. He encourages others who want to be an artist: "Don't let your fears stop you..."

Arvin's art reflects life struggles as well as his insights.

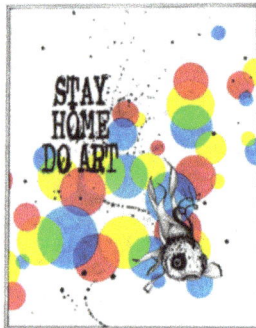

Stay Home

[When we feel] like fish trapped in their environment, the least we can do is make it colorful. I put this piece together for a community project in response to Covid-19.

Be still, and know that I am God:
I will be exalted among the heathen,
I will be exalted in the earth.
~ Psalm 46:10

Cuban Tody

Each day, the Cuban Tody, the most vibrant of the Tody family, eats 48%, or more of its own body weight. This small, mostly carnivorous bird preys on insects and lizards; with the occasional berry. To create [the painting of] this bird, I referenced seven plus photos and three different books.

Build

"What is community to me?"

...Build each other up. Support one another, both directly and indirectly. This work will build a tower of people over time; growth. Our stability comes with the focus of many. For the benefit of the community to perpetuate the community, we must focus, sometimes sacrifice.

To build a community—not a "lite" undertaking.

And let us consider one another to provoke unto love and to good works:

~ Hebrews 10:24

Juxtaposition of Depression

The many faces of depression include despair... death... with its capable touch able to affect everyone. You can be distant and personal, smile and frown, laugh and cry. The depths of the depression may be unknown.

...Open communication aids healing.

This was one of the most difficult pieces I have ever done. I had to take emotional breaks throughout the process.

Sometimes we have friends and family suffering right in front of us. There could be a daunting internal monologue that we're unaware of. It can be a real challenge to recognize what's hidden.

Past Present Future

As we constantly move from past and future, time differs for each individual. Look too far forward, you may become anxious; too far backwards, depressed. Focusing on the now, planning a future and learning from the past reduces the uncertainty...

Perspective... helped me understand I need to be more in the present. If you tilt your head, [...the painting] should show a different facial expression. It represents looking at your past experiences with a different lens enabling you to let go of trauma or grief.

Take therefore no thought for the morrow:
for the morrow shall take thought for the things of itself.
Sufficient unto the day is the evil thereof.
~ Matthew 6:34

Health & Survival...

Count Your Friends

The old man turned to me and asked,
"How many friends have you?"
"Why ten or twenty friends have I!"
And I named off just a few.
He rose quite slow with effort
And sadly shook his head,
"A lucky child you are
To have so many friends.

... "A friend is just not someone
To whom you say, 'Hello',
A friend's a tender shoulder
On which to softly cry
As well to pour your troubles down
And raise your spirits high.
"A friend is a hand to pull you up
From darkness and despair,
When all your other so-called 'friends'
Have helped to put you there.

"A true friend is an ally
Who can't be moved or bought,
A voice to keep your name alive
When others have forgot.
But most of all a friend is a heart
A strong and sturdy wall;
For from the hearts of friends
There comes the greatest love of all.

So... answer once again, my child,
How many friends have you?"
And then he stood and faced me
Awaiting my reply;
["Just one..., only one," I said. "Only one, 'tis true"]
["But... Because I'm blessed,"]
the one I have is you."

The Rule of Threes

1. How long can you survive without air?

2. How long can you survive without shelter?

3. How long can you survive without water?

The "rule of the threes" suggests broad ideas of calculations that potentially can help someone in survival situations. The rule basically states:

1. Some can but you may not survive three minutes without air...

2. Some can survive three hours but you may not without shelter...

3. Some can but you may not survive three days without water...

If a person can hold their breath for three minutes, which many cannot, they could possibly survive three minutes without air.

In a cold, cold, cold outside environment, a person can survive for approximately three hours before their body shows significant signs of hypothermia.

If a person does not have water to drink, they can likely survive three days. A person will begin to feel effects of dehydration in one day.

A person can survive about three weeks without food, however, a person will become weak if they do not eat food for three weeks.

One survivalist argues that a person may only live three seconds without thinking. This means that it only takes approximately three seconds to do something simply "stupid," horrible enough to kill them if they fail to think right.

This survivalist stresses: "...Stay calm. Don't do anything without thinking about it."

Give instruction to a wise man,
and he will be yet wiser:
teach a just man,
and he will increase in learning.
~ Proverbs 9:9

Friends Cry with Friends

Ashes, illustrated below, serves as the moderator for Job's story recounted in:

When You're Down to Your Last Donkey...
and Need to Rise Up from the Ashes.

At one point during his troubled times, Job said that he wanted to go back to the time when things were good in his life. Instead of crying with him, Job's three friends [miserable comforters] blamed him for the tragedies he suffered. Friends need friends not only in good times—but also during the bad. Sometimes, friends cry with friends.

I cry out to You, O God,
but
You do not answer.
~ Job 30:20

Why I Attend CR
Jerry Carnley

I'm ok, I thought. I don't need any help...

Prior to going to Celebrate Recovery (CR), I did not think I had a problem I could not handle myself. After attending several CR meetings and working a Step Study, however, I realized I was a total mess and did not even know it. At that time, following my divorce, I figured that part of my life had ended; that the past was over.

Well, no.., that's not true, I discovered. Through CR, I not only came to understand just how broken I was; that I needed to work through my divorce and other things in my past. In turn—I began to heal.

When someone asks me to describe my salvation experience, I often refer to my life before and after CR. Attending meetings, I learned that my recovery is a life-long process. Now, in answer to a question I often ask myself, "Why do you attend Celebrate Recovery meetings?" I realize that participating in CR did not just change my life—it began life for me.

Some people choose not to change. A few may lock into meetings for a limited time and gain some value, but then drop away. Others attend CR simply for the signature documenting their attendance and then leave. Instead of seeking and securing the help they need, some may only return the next time a judge requires them to do so.

Each day, as I pray to maintain a desire to stay stable, free, and clean, prioritizing CR meetings as well as regularly attending church helps me stay balanced.

CR not only permits me to help others who currently, or like me in my past, struggle with hurts, hang-ups, and habits. It helped me go from not realizing I was totally messed up—to getting the healing or help I so desperately needed.

Admitting *I need help...* That's even better than claiming, *I'm ok.*

God's Valentine to Us: Jesus

Every day, including Valentine's Day, offers a perfect time to remember God gave us a Valentine 2000 years ago. John 3:16 recounts that precious, priceless, perfect gift. God gave us Jesus:

For God so loved the world,
that he gave his only begotten Son,
that whosoever believeth in him
should not perish,
but have everlasting life.

Jesus gives those who believe in Him new life. Today, you have the opportunity to pray the following prayer, to be "born again." As you receive eternal life; knowing Jesus as your Savior—you have reassurance you will spend eternity in Heaven.

Lord Jesus,

I know all have sinned, and that includes me. I ask You to forgive me, come into my heart, and save me.

I receive Your gift of eternal life. I know You died for me, and shed Your blood as a sacrifice for my sins on the Cross.

I know now that I am saved, born again, and going to Heaven because of You, Jesus.

I believe with my heart, and confess with my mouth that Jesus Christ is my Lord and personal Savior.

~ Amen.

Your name: _____

Date: _____ / _____ / _____

Time: ____:_____

John B. Vennell, PhD.
Faith Community South Church
3115 Main Street
Cottondale, FL 32431

Making the Team "Picture"
Christopher L Scott

"Christopher, you won't be included in the golf team picture" my coach told me.

What...? I wondered. *How could he do this? Had I done something wrong? Made a bad decision? Been careless? Was I not trying? How could I have received a golf scholarship yet be excluded from our team's picture? Why did our coach not consider me good enough?*

I faithfully practiced my golf game and worked hard to improve. I hit hundreds of golf balls on the range every day, and spent hours doing putting drills. Nevertheless, even though I sweated profusely on hot days, and invested hours in the sand practicing my bunker shots, my coach inadvertently let me know that he thought I was not good enough. Evidently, although I tried my best according to my coach, my performance failed to measure up to the standard he wanted of me.

I did not understand my coach's concern. Of the 13 young men on the college golf team, only five of the guys qualified to travel to tournaments each week. As I started out as one of the five guys, and our coach considered me good enough to travel to the tournament each week, while eight stayed home—I wanted to protest. Even if I did not play great in every tournament, I reasoned, until now our coach had considered me good enough to be part of the traveling team. He had left eight of my fellow teammates at home.

I had peace about my golfing capabilities until all of a sudden, I started to struggle. Eventually, my coach let me know that my diminishing performance led to his decision to drop me from the five guys who traveled each week.

I had no doubt, however, that when the time came to take our team picture—I would be included. I thought, *Even if I no longer qualified as one of the five guys who traveled to tournaments, I was still part of our school's 13-guy team.*

No, I'm not, I had to admit. I had to acknowledge the reason why. My performance was not, as my coach had let me know, good enough.

Prior to this time, I regarded the golf team as my community; fellow members as my friends. We were family, and they were my family away from my biological family. I even lived with two teammates in an apartment. Now, because of our coach's decision, I felt alienated. It did not matter that I tried my best, my best effort was not good enough. My poor performance had taken me from being a part of the golf team to an outsider looking in.

Today, I thank God that, unlike my participation and inclusion in the golf team's picture, my participation in God's community is not based on performance. God does not require a standard of excellence for us to be part of His community of believers. Churches don't require you or me to "perform" or participate in a worship service, to attend a Sunday school class, or even to be a "member" of a church. As Paul wrote to the believers in Rome, "Therefore, since we have been justified through faith, we have peace with God through our Lord Jesus Christ, through whom we have gained access by faith into this grace in which we now stand" (Romans 5:1-2, NIV).

In his book, *The Bumps Are What You Climb On,* Warren Wiersbe writes:

> It is a great mistake to build your happiness on circumstances or things, because circumstances change and things have a way of wearing out and losing their value. True internal peace cannot be based on changing external things. We need something deeper and more satisfying.

The peace Jesus Christ gives proves more satisfying than that any human team can offer. "For he himself [Jesus] is our peace" (Ephesians 2:14, NIV). Christians experience peace based on Christ and faith in Him, not their performance. Christians don't make peace; they enjoy it. I am grateful that by faith I am saved and have peace with God.

Through faith in Jesus Christ, not our works nor performance, we have peace. In God's big picture, I will never be rejected. Because Jesus Christ died on the cross to pay for my sins, now on Earth as well as through eternity, I am forevermore part of Heaven's team.

Christopher L. Scott serves as senior pastor at Lakeview Missionary Church in Moses Lake, Washington. He also shares the gospel through Christian publishers distributing his articles, devotions, and pamphlets each month. More @ ChristopherLynnScott.com.

Seven Potential Perks from Working Crossword Puzzles

1. Strengthening memory

2. Exercising mind

3. Reducing onset of dementia

4. Positively distracting

5. Improving mood

6. Learning new things

7. Reducing stress

Answers to Crossword Puzzle on Page 18

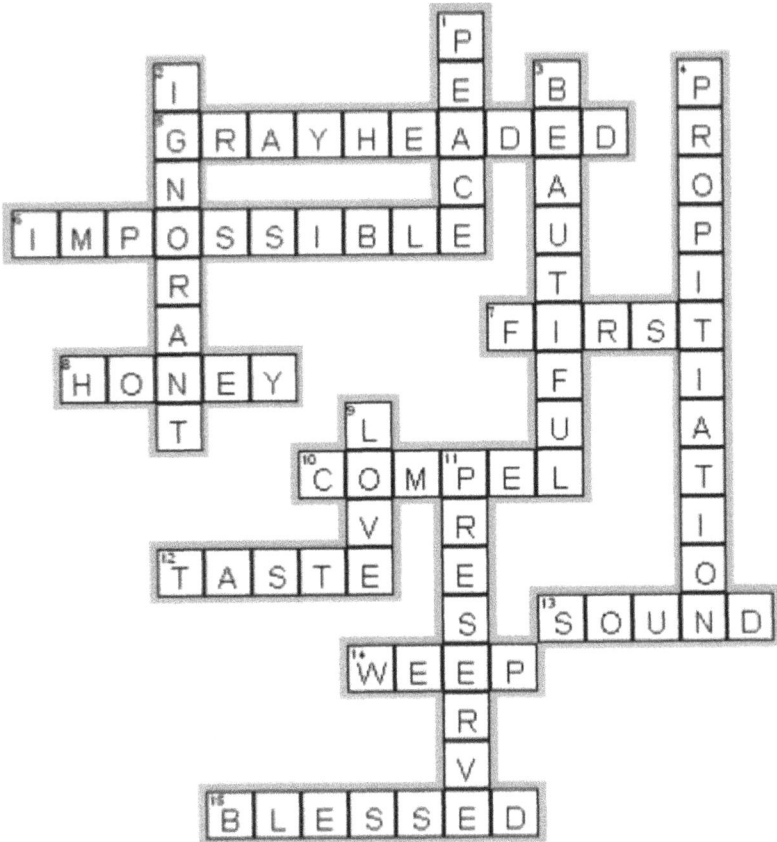

**Now concerning spiritual gifts, brethren,
I would not have you ignorant.**

~ 1 Corinthians 12:1

January 2024

Mon	Tue	Wed	Thu	Fri	Sat	Sun
1	2	3	4	5	6	7
8	9	10	11	12	13	14
15	16	17	18	19	20	21
22	23	24	25	26	27	28
29	30	31				

February 2024

Mon	Tue	Wed	Thu	Fri	Sat	Sun
			1	2	3	4
5	6	7	8	9	10	11
12	13	14	15	16	17	18
19	20	21	22	23	24	25
26	27	28	29			

March 2024

Mon	Tue	Wed	Thu	Fri	Sat	Sun
				1	2	3
4	5	6	7	8	9	10
11	12	13	14	15	16	17
18	19	20	21	22	23	24
25	26	27	28	29	30	31

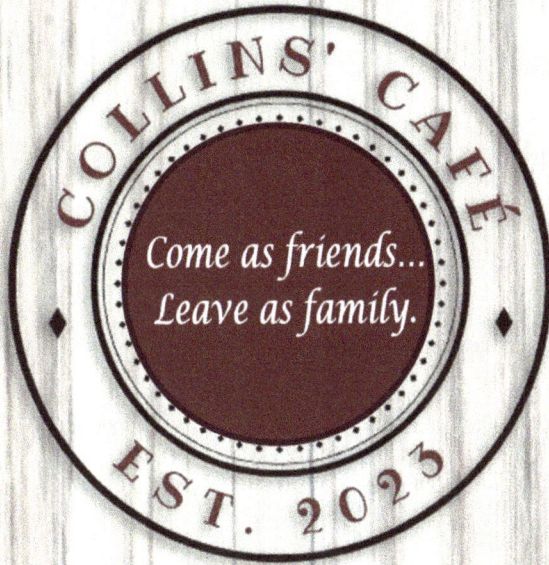

Remember...

The Lord bless thee, and keep thee:

The Lord make his face shine upon thee,
and be gracious unto thee:

The Lord lift up his countenance upon thee,
and give thee peace.

~ Numbers 6:24 – 26